AR PTS: 1.0

Martial Arts
FOR FUN!

By Kevin Carter

Content Adviser: Phil Ott, Martial Arts Instructor, Ott's Okinawan Karate, Chatham, New Jersey
Reading Adviser: Frances J. Bonacci, Reading Specialist, Cambridge, Massachusetts

COMPASS POINT BOOKS

MINNEAPOLIS, MINNESOTA

Compass Point Books
3109 West 50th Street, #115
Minneapolis, MN 55410

Visit Compass Point Books on the Internet at *www.compasspointbooks.com*
or e-mail your request to *custserv@compasspointbooks.com*

Photographs ©: Dave Mager/Index Stock, front cover (left); PhotoDisc, front cover (top right), 43 (bottom left); Comstock, front cover (bottom right); Photomondo/Getty Images, 5; Zigy Kaluzny/Getty Images, 7; Ross Whitaker/Getty Images, 9; Courtesy of Century, Incorporated, 10-11; Corbis, 13; Menachem Mandell/Index Stock, 17; Todd Powell/Index Stock, 19; Ryan McVay/Getty Images, 23; Amwell/Getty Images, 25; Duomo/Corbis, 29; G.D.T./Getty Images, 31, 35; Peter Poby/Corbis, 37; Adam Pretty/Getty Images, 39, 41; Corel, 42, 45, 47; Eyewire Images, 43 (center left), 44; Comstock Klips, 43 (top); Ingram Publishing, 43 (right).

Editor: Sandra E. Will and Meredith Phillips/Bill SMITH STUDIO
Photo Researchers: Sandra E. Will and Christie Silver/Bill SMITH STUDIO
Designer: Colleen Sweet and Brian Kobberger/Bill SMITH STUDIO

Library of Congress Cataloging-in-Publication Data
    Carter, Kevin.
    Martial arts / by Kevin Carter.
    p. cm. — (Activities for fun)
    Includes index.
    Summary: An overview of martial arts including Tae Kwon Do, Karate, Judo,
    and Kung Fu.
    ISBN 0-7565-0586-0 (hardcover)
    1. Martial arts—Juvenile literature. [1. Martial arts.] I. Title.
    II. Series.
    GV1101.35.C27 2004
    796.8—dc22
                        2003017095

Table of Contents

Note: In this book, there are two kinds of vocabulary words. Martial Arts Words to Know are words specific to martial arts. They are in **bold** and are defined on page 46. Other Words to Know are helpful words that aren't related only to martial arts. They are ***bold and italicized.*** These are defined on page 47.

Martial Arts Are Fun!

In ancient times, Asian warriors invented **martial** arts to protect their homes and families. People have used martial arts for combat and self-defense, but they are more than a means of violence and protection. They are systems that promote physical and spiritual values (see p. 19). Practitioners use their martial arts teachings in their everyday lives to find harmony and balance with the world.

People who practice martial arts, like karate and tae kwon do, spend years mastering their skills. Martial artists train to learn how to fight well and avoid injuring ***opponents.*** A good martial artist never tries to injure an opponent or fights unless it is necessary. The combination of violence and nonviolence is what makes martial arts a true "art form."

Martial arts training also helps develop the mind by teaching **concentration,** healthy living, and respect for yourself and others. If you try martial arts, your grades might improve. Your parents and teachers are likely to notice a difference, too!

Martial arts allow people to develop their mind, body, and spirit.

All Around the World

Almost every culture has developed its own form of martial arts. The first known martial arts were developed more than 4,000 years ago and came from Africa and the Middle East. The ancient Egyptians, Hebrews, and Babylonians all had fighting systems that were used by their warriors.

Most of the martial arts practiced today come from three places: China, Japan, and Korea. Other cultures have martial arts they are very proud of as well. In the United States, wrestling and boxing are popular. The French enjoy a fighting form called savate, and the descendants of Africans in Brazil practice a fighting dance form known as capoeira. This book will look at the world's most popular East Asian martial arts, such as tae kwon do (Korea), karate (Okinawa), judo (Japan), and kung fu (China).

Did You Know?

A martial arts teacher is known as a **sensei** in Japanese and a **sifu** or **laoshi** in Chinese. **Sabunnim** is a Korean word for teacher.

Which One Is for You?

There are hundreds of different martial arts. These arts can be classified into several categories. Some use weapons. Most are unarmed arts, which means they use no weapons.

The major categories of unarmed arts are **grappling** arts and striking arts. Grappling arts, such as judo or high school wrestling, use **throws, armlocks,** and **pins** to control an attacker or opponent. Striking arts, such as karate, tae kwon do, and boxing, use mostly punches and kicks.

Some arts use both grappling and striking elements. For example, Japan's aikido and Chinese kung fu use both elements. Some arts are done as forms of exercise rather than forms of fighting. These are called **soft arts.**

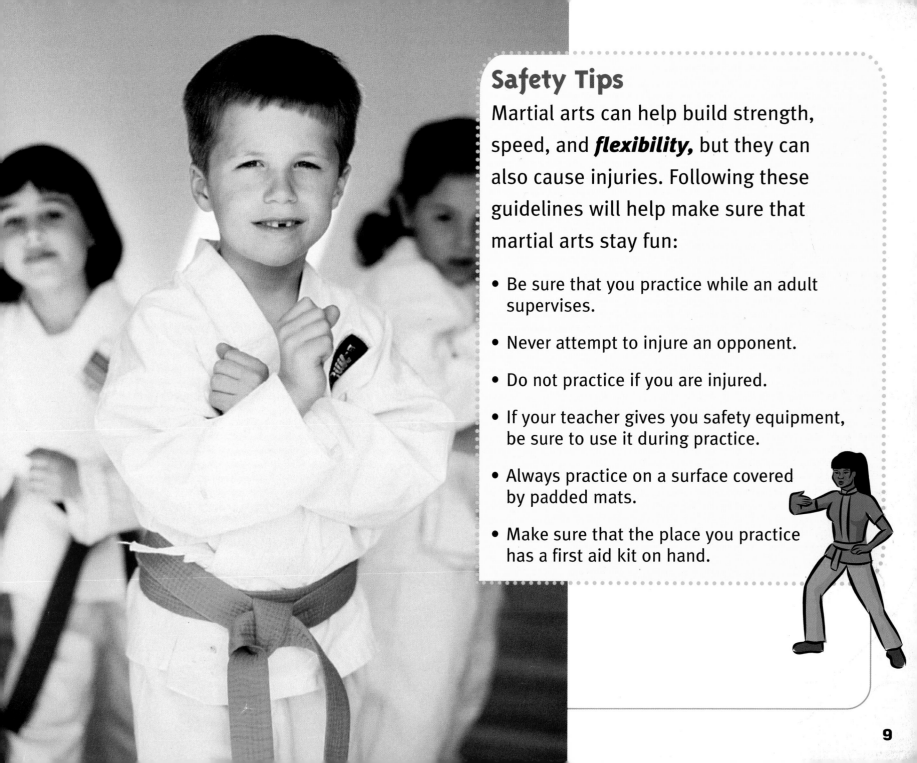

Safety Tips

Martial arts can help build strength, speed, and *flexibility,* but they can also cause injuries. Following these guidelines will help make sure that martial arts stay fun:

- Be sure that you practice while an adult supervises.

- Never attempt to injure an opponent.

- Do not practice if you are injured.

- If your teacher gives you safety equipment, be sure to use it during practice.

- Always practice on a surface covered by padded mats.

- Make sure that the place you practice has a first aid kit on hand.

Get in Gear

Regardless of which martial art you practice, looking good and being comfortable and safe all go together.

Each martial art has its own style, but in many—such as karate, tae kwon do, and judo—the participants wear a **gi,** a loose fitting cotton or canvas uniform in which it is easy to move. Wearing gis allows opponents to grab one another without tearing their clothing. A gi is often white. In judo, the gi is sometimes blue. The gi is tied with a belt or sash.

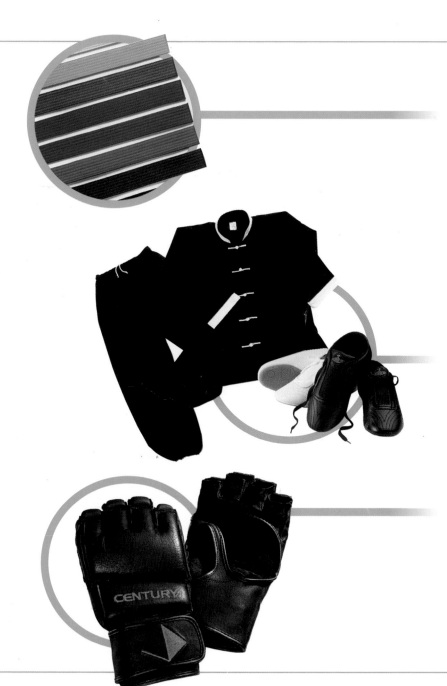

The color of the belt shows the level of skill. Beginners wear white belts. Over time and with a lot of hard work, one can advance to yellow, green, blue, red, and black. A black or black and red belt often means a teacher or an expert.

In most styles of kung fu, competitors wear a loose-fitting and sturdy cotton or silk uniform with flat rubber-soled shoes.

At competitions, tae kwon do practitioners wear gloves and a mouthpiece.

What It Is

Have you ever pretended to be a karate expert? When people think of martial arts, they often think of karate first. The word karate means "empty hand" in Japanese. People doing karate fight mostly with their hands and feet, without weapons.

Karate as we know it today came from Okinawa, a small former island kingdom, which is now part of Japan. When the Japanese first occupied Okinawa in the late 1400s, Zen Buddhist monks, who had a large amount of contact with China, developed karate to fight the invaders. In the early 20th century, Gichin Funakoshi, an Okinawan, brought karate to the mainland of Japan.

Karate was one of the first arts to come to North America and has been the subject of many movies, cartoons, and TV shows, like "Dragon Ball Z" and "The Karate Kid." As a result, karate is one of the most widely known and popular martial arts in the United States, as well as Japan and Okinawa.

These competitors perform the high block (left) and the reverse punch (right) during their karate fight.

How to Do It

Beginning **karatekas,** or karate competitors, learn the three basic stances, or positions: left, right, and front. The front (shown on pg. 15) is the most important because it is the most frequently used position. Karatekas also learn a series of five kicks, blocks, and punches. Blocks are important because defensive skills are the most necessary part of all fighting arts. People cannot fight unless they can protect themselves!

In order to master the basics of karate, trainees learn a series of **kata**—or karate techniques. They are performed in a certain order against an imaginary opponent. Kata contain many kicks and punches and are practiced over and over again so that a trainee memorizes all of the basic moves.

Step 1: Begin with both feet facing forward and a shoulders' width apart.

Step 2: Keep your left foot in place. Then, move your right leg straight back behind you, while bending your left knee. Both feet should stay on the floor. Next, straighten out your right leg. Your left knee should be in a straight line with your ankle.

Step 3: Make fists with your hands. Then, raise your left arm out in front of you above your left leg. Turn your right fist palm-side up, bringing your arm up by your side. Your fist should be resting next to your waist.

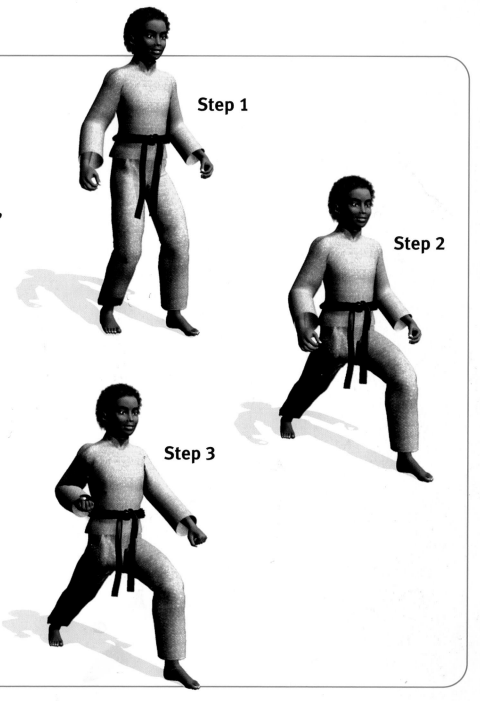

Step 1

Step 2

Step 3

Matches & Competitions

There are many forms of competition in karate. Kata competition, as you just learned, has a series of karate techniques performed in a certain order against an imaginary opponent. In point competitions, fighters aim to kick or punch a particular place, or point, on the other competitor while the opponent tries to defend himself or herself.

During a point competition, two competitors wear gis and shin protectors. One wears red gloves, and the other one wears blue gloves. They face off on a woven fighting mat. The fighters bow and approach each other. They try to find an opportunity to punch or kick without injuring the opponent. A single-scoring punch or kick scores one point. Some combinations score two or three points. Youth competitors fight one two-minute round.

Another kind of karate competition is fought in a ring similar to a boxing ring. The rules are like boxing, too. A fighter can win by knockout or by making the most effective kicks or punches. To prepare for competition, a karateka trains in a room or building called a **dojo.**

A girl performs a technique in a competition.

What It Is

Tae kwon do is one of the most amazing arts to watch. In Korean, the words tae kwon do mean "the art of kicking or smashing with the hand and the foot, while jumping and flying." When you see fighters flying through the air with legs held high, breaking boards with their feet, chances are they are doing tae kwon do.

Tae kwon do practitioners say tae kwon do is a violent art, but it was developed for nonviolent purposes. The art was developed in April 1955. Martial arts masters from all over Korea came together to develop a new art by combining the many different arts that Koreans practiced.

Tae kwon do beginners first learn basic punches and kicks. When they get past white-belt level, the teacher begins to include lessons about the human body. More advanced students of tae kwon do are also expected to apply the **principles** of tae kwon do in their daily life.

PRINCIPLES OF TAE KWON DO

Etiquette	the rules for polite behavior
Modesty	politeness regarding your own abilities
Perseverance	the ability to keep trying through difficulties
Self-control	the ability to control your own behavior
Invincible spirit	enthusiasm or force that is impossible to overcome because of great skill

How to Do It

Tae kwon do is well known for its flashy kicking movements. Basic kicking moves, like the front kick (shown on p. 21), are not difficult to learn. More advanced kicks require more experienced training. Practitioners learn the standing and jumping versions of many types of kicks, such as the roundhouse and side. They also use many spinning kicks that are powerful and performed quickly.

People who study tae kwon do learn a set of basic stances. The ready, guard, and defensive stances are the most common. They also learn how to hold their hands to attack and defend. Like karate, tae kwon do uses the "empty hand" method, which means no weapons. Practitioners use blocks, punches, and other types of hand strikes instead.

Step 1: Start with both feet facing forward. Your left foot should be slightly in front of your right.

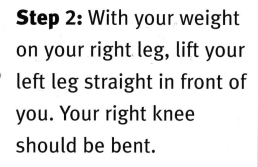

Step 2: With your weight on your right leg, lift your left leg straight in front of you. Your right knee should be bent.

Step 3: To strike a target, quickly bend at the knee and hit with your foot. Use the ball of your left foot as the kicking surface.

Matches & Competitions

A tae kwon do **sparring** match is fought in a ring that measures 26 feet (8 meters) square. In a sparring match, points are scored by kicking or punching designated target areas. Competitors can win by making strikes that score one, two, or three points. Matches have two rounds, and each round lasts two minutes. A **_referee,_** four judges, and two jurors supervise the matches.

Competitors can hit only the front of the body between the opponent's waist and neck. No punches can be aimed at the head, but competitors can kick the head. They cannot attack the knees or throw their opponent down. If the score is tied, or if no one has scored a point, the referee and judges can decide the winner based on which opponent fought better.

Patterns, known as **hyung,** are another way to compete in tae kwon do. In this version of the martial art, a panel of judges determines who has done his or her patterns the best.

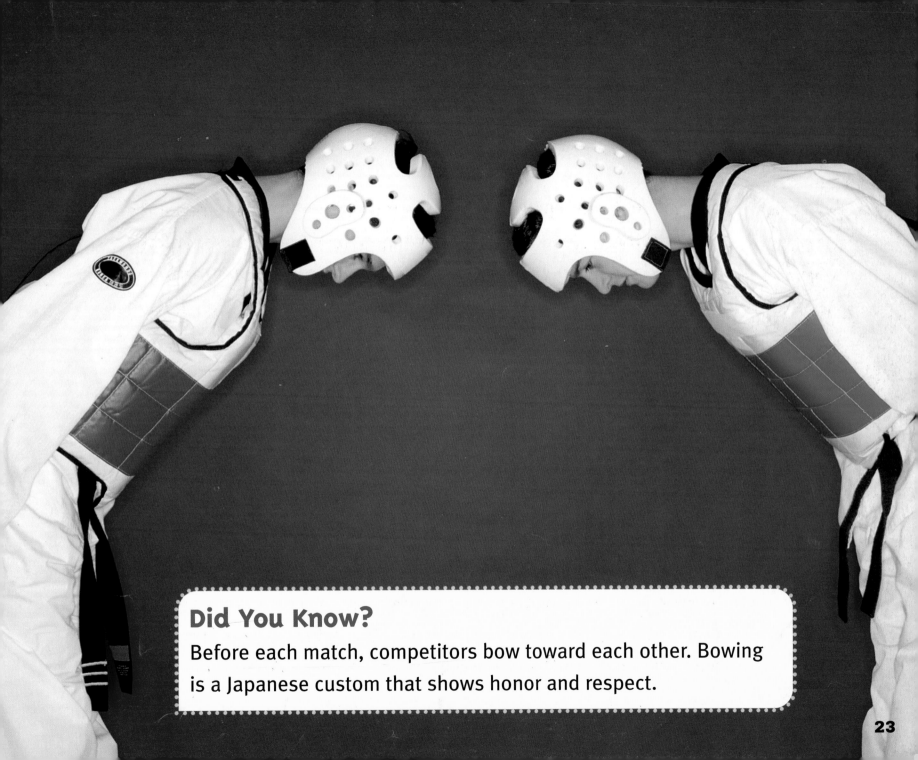

Did You Know?

Before each match, competitors bow toward each other. Bowing is a Japanese custom that shows honor and respect.

What It Is

In Japanese, the word judo means "the gentle way." Judo is a grappling art in which opponents use motion and *leverage* to throw each other to the ground. In judo, you may also learn wrestling techniques that allow you to hold down, choke, or armlock another person.

Although you can sometimes see spectacular throws in judo, strength is not the most important quality you must develop. The two central ideas behind judo are "maximum *efficiency*," and "*mutual* welfare and benefit, or good effect." This means using body position, footwork, and leverage, not size and strength. In judo, skill is an important part of defeating an opponent. **Judokas** use small movements and angles to outsmart their opponents.

This woman uses her body position to throw her opponent over her hip and to the ground.

How to Do It

Did you know that there is a correct way to fall in judo? The first thing judokas learn when they go to judo class is how to fall. Since judo includes many throwing techniques, it is very important to learn how to fall properly so that people do not get hurt. The series of falls that are taught in judo are called **ukemi.** Judokas learn to fall backward, forward, and to each side. Look at the next page to learn the backward fall.

There are two basic types of skills used in judo: throwing and ne-waza, or mat work. In throwing, participants learn how to upset their opponent's balance by pushing or pulling on their body.

Ne-waza skills help control an opponent after throwing him or her to the ground. Judo students can learn other mat work moves, such as pins and chokes, to keep an opponent down on the mat.

Step 1: To practice, stand on a mat with your legs forward and your arms stretched out at shoulder height, palms facing down. Remember! You should always practice on a mat for safety.

Step 2: Fall backward, bending your neck, arching your back, and raising your legs. Tuck your chin into your chest to protect your head.

Step 3: Slap the mat hard with your hands and arms at the same moment that your back hits the mat. Your arms should be angled away from your body. Finally, sit up by lowering your legs and return to the original standing position.

Step 1   Step 2   Step 3

Matches & Competitions

In order to practice judo, the judoka must have a soft, matted surface on which to fall. The mat for judo competitions is traditionally just under 48 feet (15 m) by 48 feet (15 m). That is the area of eight Japanese **tatami mats.**

Before a judo match begins, competitors must walk up to the mat in bare feet and bow. Shoes should never be worn on the mat. Then, they bow to the referee and to their opponents. During the match, competitors try to throw their opponents to the ground and pin them.

A judo match is won when one competitor scores **ippon,** or one point. Waza-ari, a nearly completed throw, or a 20-second hold-down, counts as half of a point. Yuko is a quarter-point, and koka is one-eighth of a point. If a competitor has one waza-ari, that beats out any number of yuko or koka his or her opponent might have.

A person can score ippon in three ways: a completed throw, a 25-second hold-down, or any hold that forces the other competitor to submit by tapping his or her hands on the mat or the other competitor.

Did You Know?

Judo competition has no rounds. A match can last six to 20 minutes, depending on the format.

What It Is

Kung fu is one of the most popular arts in the world. The Chinese words kung fu have been translated as "skill from effort." The major reason for that is the popularity of Chinese martial arts movies and movie stars. Bruce Lee, Jackie Chan, Sammo Hung, Chow Yun-fat, and Michelle Yeoh are all kung fu experts.

Kung fu is one of the oldest Chinese fighting arts. The first people to use kung fu in China were Buddhist monks at the Shaolin Temple more than 1,500 years ago. Kung fu has hundreds of different styles. Within the category of kung fu, there are **hard styles,** soft styles, and those that use weapons. Most styles of kung fu use circular movements in their punches, throws, and kicks. Some styles, such as shuai-chiao, include many grappling movements.

Different Styles of Kung Fu

In each different form of kung fu, participants have different objectives, or goals. In tai chi, the goal is to develop an internal power called "chi." In wing chun, the goal is to develop a hands-based fighting style that is direct and confined to a small area. Praying mantis is a graceful, medium-tempo style with movements that are a lot like those done by animals, such as grasshoppers and snakes.

This kung fu fighter is performing the beginning movements of his form. Kung fu has forms that are like karate's katas.

How to Do It

Kung fu beginners learn a series of circular movements with their arms and legs. Unlike karate and other striking arts, the kung fu fighter will learn combinations of kicks, punches, and **sweeps** from the very beginning. Some of the basic stances of kung fu are known as the **horse,** bow and arrow, cat, guard, and seven star. Other forms of martial arts also have stances with these same names, but they are slightly different. In kung fu, the positions are much lower to the ground than in other martial arts.

People who study kung fu learn many moves that involve going from one stance to another by spinning on the balls of their feet and jumping slightly off the ground. They also learn to roll forward and backward and how to breathe properly. Kung fu fighters are known for their ability to move quickly and silently.

Here is a description of how to perform the cat stance, which allows you to strike quickly like a cat:

Step 1: Start with your feet facing forward. Turn your right foot and touch your heels together: Your feet should take the position of 2 o'clock, as if they were the hands of a clock.

Step 2: Move your left foot forward about 10 inches (25 centimeters). Then, raise your left heel 4 to 5 inches (10 to 13 cm) off the ground. Both of your legs should be bent.

Step 3: Shift all of your weight to your right leg. Then, place your hands in front of you in fists, palm-sides facing in (like a boxer).

Step 1

Step 2

Step 3

Matches & Competitions

In some forms of kung fu, like tai chi, there are no grading systems or competitions. In point competition, each opponent wears traditional kung fu clothing with standard boxing gloves, chest protectors, knee and foot pads, mouth guards, and other protective gear. Fighters enter a 26-foot (8-m) ring, called a lei tai, which is usually elevated 24 inches (61 cm) off the ground. They stand 15 feet (5 m) apart. Before the fight, fighters greet the referee and their opponent with a palm-fist salute.

In a kung fu competition, fighters can hit their opponent in the head, upper body, or legs. All front and back punches are legal. Sweeps and kicks are legal, unless they are meant to injure the opponent. Techniques can score from one to three points. Kung fu fights can be won by points, knockouts, or by the decision of the referee.

Kung fu fighters also compete in no-contact competitions. In these types of competitions, fighters do not wear protective equipment.

Across the Globe

Most martial arts originated in Asia, but other nations and cultures have developed their own arts as well. Bruce Lee's Jeet Kune Do, originally developed in the United States, and Kajukenbo from Hawaii are martial arts that combine more than one original art into something new.

Brazilian Jiu-Jitsu is this type of martial art, too. In fact, it is among the fastest-growing martial arts in the world. Another Brazilian martial art is capoeira, a popular dancelike art that came from Africans who were taken to Brazil as slaves during the 1500s. When you watch, it seems similar to break dancing! This is because the enslaved people pretended to be dancing while they were really learning to protect themselves.

Tai chi (China), hapkido (Korea), savate (France), and sumo (Japan, Korea, and Mongolia) are other popular forms of martial arts.

Many people prefer to practice some types of martial arts, like tai chi, outside in the natural environment.

Go for the Gold

Ever since 1896, at the first modern Olympic Games in Athens, Greece, some of the best martial artists in the world have had an opportunity to show their skills. At first, just one form of wrestling, greco-roman, was included. In 1920, boxing was added. In 1964, judo *debuted* in Tokyo, and tae kwon do debuted in Barcelona in 1992. In 2004, women's wrestling was introduced.

In judo, men and women compete in seven different classes. A person's weight determines his or her class. At the Olympics, men and women compete in eight different tae kwon do classes. The top three finishers in each class win a gold, silver, or bronze medal.

Did You Know?
The first U.S. judo team in 1964 represented America's diversity well, with one Native American, one Japanese American, one African American, and one European American.

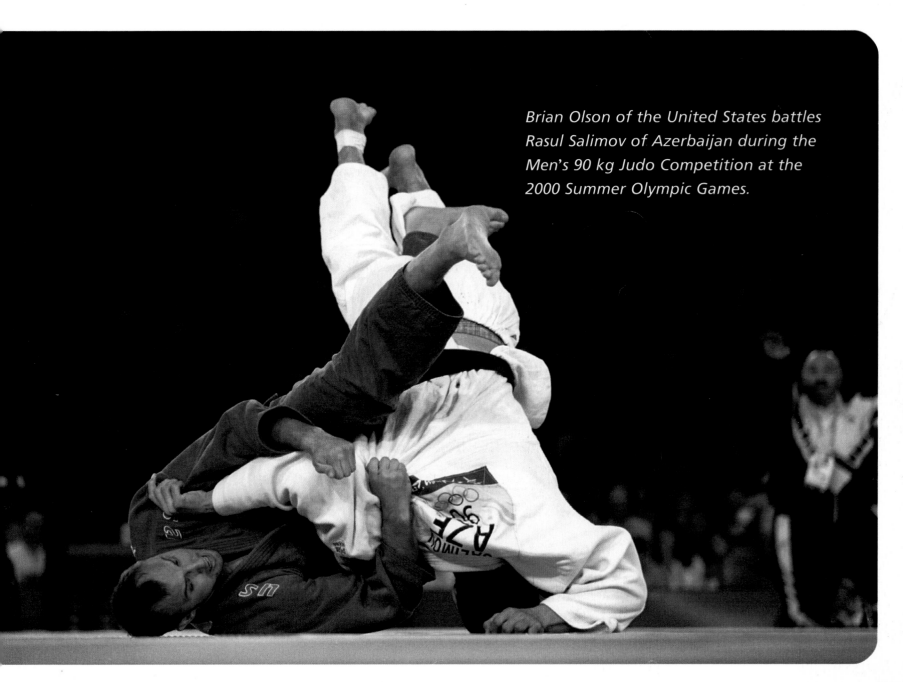

Brian Olson of the United States battles Rasul Salimov of Azerbaijan during the Men's 90 kg Judo Competition at the 2000 Summer Olympic Games.

Let the Games Begin!

In addition to the Olympics, martial arts practitioners participate in many other types of competitions. Boxing, wrestling, judo, and tae kwon do are part of the Pan American Games, a competition for North, Central, and South America, as well as the Caribbean. The World Games, which are held every four years, provide another opportunity for martial arts competitors. Athletes from around the world also compete in the Commonwealth Games, which are held every four years.

The largest single martial arts competition in the United States is held every spring in Columbus, Ohio. It includes the Arnold (Schwarzenegger) Classic Gracie Jiu Jitsu Gi Competition and Submission Championships. The Arnold Traditional Karate Championship also takes place at the same time.

People of all ages and skill levels compete in other martial arts tournaments around the world. Would you like to compete some day?

Catherine Roberge (left), Samantha Lowe, Amanda Costello, and Sisilia Nasiga received medals in the Women's Judo 70 kg Final at the 2002 Commonwealth Games.

What Happened When?

| 2000 B.C. | 100 B.C. | 500 A.D | 1500 | 1629 | 1850 | 1880 | 1920 | 1940 | 1950 |

2000 B.C. Grappling figurines from this period of time have been found in Egypt and Babylonia.

100 B.C. Figures in karate-like poses are carved on the walls of a Korean temple.

500 A.D. The Shaolin Temple is built in China by kung fu-practicing monks.

1500s African slaves are brought to Brazil and bring the new martial art, capoeira, with them.

1629 Capoeira masters found Palmares, a society of runaway African slaves in the interior of Brazil.

1853 Sumo wrestlers greet Admiral Perry's soldiers and sailors in Tokyo Bay and demonstrate their strength by lifting rice on the docks. Admiral Perry was the American responsible for opening up trade between Japan and the rest of the world.

1882 Jigoro Kano invents judo and establishes the Kodokan, the first judo academy in Tokyo, Japan.

1922 Gichin Funakoshi establishes Shotokan karate, a combination of all Okinawan karate styles, in Japan.

1940 Bruce Lee, the kung fu expert who became the first martial arts movie star, is born in San Francisco.

1942 Sensei Morihei Ueshiba first uses the word aikido to describe his art.

1955 Korean hapkido and hwarangdo masters unite to form the new art of tae kwon do.

Japan

| 1960 | 1970 | 1980 | 1990 | 2000 |

1960 Cassius Clay, later to be known as Muhammad Ali, wins Olympic gold in boxing.

1964 Judo becomes an official Olympic sport at the Summer Olympic Games.

1971 A television drama called "Kung Fu" is a huge hit in the United States.

1988 Tae kwon do is a demonstration sport at the Olympic Games.

1990 Ryoko Tamura, at age 15, becomes the youngest woman to win a Japanese national judo championship.

1992 Half middleweight Yael Arad becomes Israel's first Olympic medalist, when she takes a silver medal in her weight class in judo.

1993 Chad Rowan, known as Akebono, becomes the first non-Japanese sumo grand champion.

1999 "Leka" Vieira becomes the first woman to receive a black belt in Brazilian jiu-jitsu.

2000 Lucia Rijker, who has a black belt in judo and is the Dutch kickboxing champion, is designated best female boxer in the world, pound for pound.

2002 Rie Tsuhiji, who weighs 340 pounds (154 kilograms) wins the All-Japan Women's Sumo Championships for the third time.

Martial Arts Trivia

Jackie Chan weighed 12 pounds (5 kg) at birth!

Bruce Lee appeared in his first movie when he was 3 months old. The movie, "Golden Gate Girl," was done in Chinese. Lee played a baby girl, held in his father's arms.

Kung fu movie stars Jackie Chan, Yuen Biao, and Sammo Hung all graduated from the same school in China—the Beijing Opera School.

In 1924, the martial art of savate was the first art to be included in an Olympic demonstration.

Vladimir Putin, president of Russia, has a black belt in judo. He occasionally allows himself to be thrown by kids studying judo, sometimes even while wearing a tie!

In Japan, it is considered good luck if a mother or father lets their baby be held by a sumo wrestler. If a sumotori holds your baby, it is believed the child will grow up big and strong.

Many of the techniques of all kung fu styles were developed after Buddhist monks and other fighters watched how animals moved.

U.S. Senator Ben Nighthorse Campbell of Colorado has a black belt in judo. Campbell competed on the 1964 U.S. Olympic team.

Martial Arts Words to Know

armlock: a tight grip around an opponent's arm or arms so that they cannot move

dojo: martial arts training place (Japanese)

gi: a judo, karate, or tae kwon do uniform

grapple: to grab hold of and struggle

hard style, or hard art: style of martial arts used for defense or fighting

horse stance: a wide, low stance that forms the basis for many styles of kung fu

hyung: patterns of kicking and punching movements in tae kwon do

ippon: a winning point in judo

judoka: a judo competitor

karateka: a karate competitor

kata: a pre-arranged series of movements using blocks, punches, kicks, and strikes

laoshi: Chinese word for teacher

martial: warlike and fierce

pin: a fall in which an opponent's shoulders are made to touch the mat

sabunnim: Korean word for teacher

sensei: Japanese word for teacher

sifu: Chinese word for teacher

soft art, or soft style: describes a martial art used for exercise instead of fighting

sparring: practicing martial arts using light blows

sweep: a fast-kicking motion where someone uses his or her foot low on the opponent's leg to knock the foot out from under the opponent

tatami mat: a woven straw mat

throw: a movement that causes an opponent to fall to the ground

ukemi: falls in judo

GLOSSARY
Other Words to Know

Here are definitions for some of the words used in this book:

concentration: the ability to direct thought or effort toward a particular task or idea

debuted: first appeared

efficiency: the ability to do something well without wasted energy

flexibility: to be able to bend or move easily

leverage: the action of gaining an advantage

mutual: shared by two or more people

opponent: a person faced in a competition

principle: the idea behind or way that something works

referee: an official who oversees the play in a sport or game

Where to Learn More

AT THE LIBRARY

Dunphy, Michael J. *The Kids' Karate Book & Karate Belt*. New York: Workman Publishing, 1999.

Knotts, Bob. *Martial Arts*. New York: Scholastic, 2000.

Olson, Stuart Alve and Gregory Crawford. *Tai Chi for Kids: Move with the Animals: Eight Simple Tai Chi Movements Parents Can Teach Their Children for Health, Imagination, and Play*. Santa Fe, NM: Bear & Co., 2001.

Yates, Keith and Bryan Robbins. *Tae Kwon Do for Kids*. New York: Sterling Publications, 1998.

ON THE ROAD

International Boxing Hall of Fame
1 Hall of Fame Drive
Canastota, NY 13032
315/697-7095
www.ibhof.com

Gracie Jiu-Jitsu Academy and Museum
1951 W. Carson St.
Torrance, CA 90501
310/782-1309
www.gracieacademy.com

ON THE WEB

For more information on *martial arts,* use FactHound to track down Web sites related to this book.

1. Go to www.compasspointbooks.com/facthound
2. Type in this book ID: 0756505860
3. Click on the *FETCH IT* button.

Your trusty FactHound will fetch the best Web sites for you!

INDEX

ABOUT THE AUTHOR

Kevin L. Carter is a freelance writer who has extensive martial arts experience as a competitor, writer, and broadcaster. A former arts critic and sportswriter at the Philadelphia Inquirer, Carter's articles have appeared in many newspapers and magazines around the world. He fought in three World Sumo Championships, has competed in dual meets for the U.S. National Sumo Team, and has coached Puerto Rico's national team. A graduate of Harvard University and the University of Hawaii, Kevin loves cooking and grappling. He lives near Princeton, New Jersey, with his wife and three children.